a book of
women's altars

a book of
women's altars

how to create
sacred spaces
for art, worship,
solace, celebration

nancy brady cunningham
photography by denise geddes

Red Wheel
Boston, MA / York Beach, ME

First published in 2002 by
Red Wheel/Weiser, LLC
York Beach, ME
With offices at:
368 Congress Street
Boston, MA 02210
www.redwheelweiser.com

Library of Congress Cataloging-in-Publication Data

Cunningham, Nancy Brady
A book of women's altars : how to create sacred spaces for art, worship, solace, celebration/Nancy Brady Cunningham; photographs by Dennis Geddes.
    p. cm.
Includes bibliographical references.
  ISBN 1-59003-011-7 (alk. paper)
1. Women—Religious life. 2. Rites and ceremonies. I. Title.
  BL625.7 .C85 2002
  291.3'7—dc21

                    2002004459

Typeset in Matrix

Printed in Canada
TCP
09 08 07 06 05 04 03 02
 8 7 6 5 4 3 2 1

contents

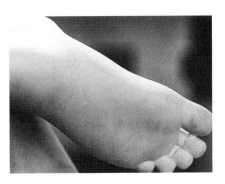

foreword

The word "altar" derives from words meaning "a high place" (think "altitude"). In the
past, altars were indeed elevated—symbolically as well as literally—above our mundane and ordinary lives, for spirituality was separated from life rather than a living,
breathing part of it. An altar was what you encountered at church on Sunday: a space
set apart, approachable only by the elect. What occurred there was meaningful but
mysterious, and when it was over, we all went back to those mundane ordinary lives.

   If there is one thing that the women's spiritual revolution challenges, it is the dual-
istic thinking that divides spirit from body, holy from secular, priest from person.
Seeing difference is not the problem: the problem is an implied hierarchy, a worldview
that says that not only are priests separate from ordinary people, but they are better,
holier, more spiritual. An important part of this dualism has been to imagine woman on
the side of the body—even, in extreme cases, of the devil—so that the idea of a woman
priest becomes an impossible self-contradiction.

   As women seek a spiritual vision that embraces rather than rejects all of life, we
have begun to re-invigorate our lives by eliminating the false barriers between
"church" and "home," between "sacred" and "profane." The altar that we once encoun-

tered for one holy hour each Sunday now finds its way into our offices, our bedrooms, our kitchens. No longer elevated above our daily lives, the altar now expresses the way spirit dances like wind through this world. As simple as an arrangement of fresh flowers or sea-polished stones, the altar speaks to us in the language of dreams, of visions, of art, revealing the beauty and meaning within each sacred moment.

Nancy Brady Cunningham and Denise Geddes do more in this book than document the possibilities of the contemporary altar. They also show the way to a vigorous new spiritual life, one that freshly images the relation of self and the universe. Theirs is a simple but powerful message: take communion at your dining table; bless yourself at your dresser; confess to your journal and forgive yourself; baptize each new aspect of your life in the fresh water of your own power. Such simple but revolutionary personal sacraments create beauty and sanctity in these, our precious fleeting lives.

Patricia Monaghan

acknowledgments

Nancy:

A very special thank you to my daughter-in-law Melissa, whose computer skills and cheerful willingness to help brought this book to life.

Warm thanks to my circle sisters — our group altars are a constant inspiration to me.

I owe a great debt of thanks to everyone in the Poetry Workshop at the Boston Center for Adult Education, with special gratitude to Ottone M. Riccio, who facilitates the workshop with warmth and humor.

Loving thanks to Denise Geddes and Sandy Borges for their friendship.

I'm grateful to my husband Ed for keeping the hearth fires burning while I write. Thanks to my children, Devin and Cara, for their love which always encourages me.

Denise:

Thanks to Marshall Zidel, who first showed me how to shoot black and white film and to the Essex Photographic Workshop, the source of much technical knowledge for me.

Gratitude and love to Nancy Brady Cunningham for involving me in this wonderful project.

Thank you to my mother, my sisters, and my brother for their continued support and encouragement of my photographic work.

introduction:
a woman's place

When a woman creates an altar, she re-collects the scattered parts of herself, reconnects with her inner beauty, and reflects on the Essential Feminine within her psyche. Her altar represents her essential self and becomes a visual metaphor for her woman-spirit. A woman's altar is the bridge between her inner world and the world of form. It is where she is free to capture and display the shapes, the shades, and the substance of her invisible essence. Once she has created the altar, a woman depends on it to tell the story of her inner life, piece by piece. The altar provides a creative, spiritual, and aesthetic way to see the story of her inner life. It is a place of her own where she can take time to make sense of the insane pace of life, where she can find the space to simplify, where she can just sit and stare.

The altar becomes a place where a woman can commune with both the personal and the cosmic aspects of herself, where she can both dance with the Divine and imbue every aspect of her personal life with sacredness, where she can both reclaim her power and revel in her innate beauty.

An altar can be used in many ways:

to say thank you to the powers that be

to celebrate Mother Nature in all Her guises

to seek spiritual wisdom

to honor the ancestors

to offer up struggles

to receive creative inspiration

to dialogue with the deeper part of her being

to honor her body

This is a partial list—the uses of the altar are limited only by a woman's imagination!

The altar is a canvas on which a woman paints various and often contradictory portraits of herself: One month she's in touch with her artist's soul, the next she's considering taking courses in computer science. One week she's intent on mediating her family's problems, the next she's boldly, bluntly expressing her opinions to all concerned. One day she's all gentle warmth, the next she's a sizzling siren. The various altars reflect and honor all the many selves she harbors within her psyche.

The simple act of displaying her hidden aspects has two powerful effects. First, the woman feels whole as each part of herself has its "moment in the sun" on her altar. Second, the woman embraces her uniqueness as she witnesses her personal inner beauty. An altar can be an actualization of a vision—in this instance, a vision of a valuable, powerful person who lives according to her own standards, irrespective of society's view of her.

Creating an altar is a life-affirming act in a world seemingly hell-bent on destruction. The altar provides comfort by acclaiming, through its very existence, that the woman is an integral part of the living cosmos, that her life is touched by the same mysterious rhythm bringing the seasons round and round, and that beneath the apparent chaos of her life an ordering force beats quietly. The altar becomes an exquisite manifestation of the healing energy of integration. Altar-making clears a path through the clutter of her world and creates a place where the feminine force in her life is visible, where she is free to make her inner journey, where healing is abundant.

1 balance between earth and sky:

what is an altar?

In the most casual sense, an altar is a place where you arrange an assortment of special things:

a shelf of treasured family photos

a desk holding mementos from a summer holiday

a dresser top displaying a jewelry box collection

a mantel trimmed with seasonal decorations

a dressing table covered with perfume bottles

a hearth and its collection of tools: shovel, poker, bellows, broom

a bureau with a basket of brightly colored scarves arranged beside a framed drawing

of a seascape.

Nothing on any of these altars is of great monetary worth, so why are these things valued? Because they are meaningful to the altar-maker. The objects radiate energy simply because they've been placed apart, arranged, and lifted up for all to see. Although their creators might not consider them altars, they do qualify as such by virtue of their creators' intent to bring together objects that recall people, places, and experiences that are special to them. However, not every collection of special things can be considered an altar. "Arrangement" is the key word here. If someone left an empty soda can among the mementos on your shelf and you didn't notice, chances are you have a cluttered shelf, not an altar.

An altar is a mixture of various energies. For example, an altar dedicated to the first stirrings of spring might include a bowl of fresh water. The water represents both the spirit of spring (inherent in the thawing of ponds and lakes) and the cleansing property of water (signifying the inner renewal that people often experience as this season arrives). In addition, a hyacinth might be placed on the altar in memory of a beloved grandmother who favored this spring bloom above all others. Artistic energy could be present in the form of a hand-crafted clay ladle glazed a beautiful spring green. These three items draw together different energies on the altar: the spiritual energy of spring's purifying waters, the emotional energy of love for a deceased grandmother, and the artistic energy of a potter.

An altar may be kept indoors or outdoors. Outdoor altars are particularly appropriate to honor nature because they can be thought of as a middle ground between earth and sky. A tree stump is a "found" outdoor altar since it is a raised surface you might come across anywhere. You place objects on it that speak of the beauty (wildflowers), or the regenerative power (molted snakeskin), or the permanence (stones), or the delicacy (robin's egg) of nature. If the tree stump is not on your property, leave the objects set up for other hikers to contemplate. If the tree stump is on your land, visit this natural altar every day, observing how the forces of sun, wind, and rain change it over time.

A flower garden is an outdoor altar, a piece of land set aside as a meeting place for the four elements: water (rain), fire (sun), earth (soil), and air (wind).

Each flower is a mini altar—

its face a raised surface lifted skyward

in honor of Mother Nature.

Time spent making, embellishing, and dismantling an altar—as well as time spent meditating, musing, or simply sitting there—might be considered wasteful by worldly standards. Why? Because there's nothing to strive for, no goal to attain, no money to be made, no competition to win! As you enshrine that which is of value to you, you continuously strengthen your contact with the deeper self, and this connection generates a more authentic you—a vital, confident woman who approaches the world and its problems with courage and a fresh perspective. Your altar helps you balance yourself. It gives you energy and helps you decide which life path to follow. It becomes the place where you perform ceremonies to honor Mother Nature, your ancestors, your creativity, and even the mundane chores of your daily life. Your altar enhances your dreams.

An altar is a place you go to reclaim your woman's intuition. This place says to the busy, rational mind, "Quiet down—let the deeper, wiser woman within you speak!" Over time your view of yourself and your place in the world shifts.

The altar becomes a sacred space because you place symbols of your true self on it. As you sit before the altar, these symbols act as mirrors reflecting your deeper self.

The peace you've invested in your

altar now radiates back to you.

You see yourself differently while looking in the mirror, and, in time, you find the courage to be this authentic self more frequently in the world.

Both you and your altar give and receive energy. For example, if you've created an altar devoted to inner peace, you have spent time and thought gathering together objects which symbolize peace for you. As you put the altar together this collection of things creates an almost palpable sensation of calm. This tranquillity is separate and not dependent on your inner state; therefore, the simple act of sitting before the altar when you are feeling frazzled will quiet your agitated emotions. Why? Because the altar absorbed your peaceful vibes when you were in a less harried frame of mind.

There is an individual design for each person's life hidden within the unconscious or deeper mind. Keeping an altar is one way to tap into this unconscious wisdom and discover the personal blueprint for your life. The road most consistent with your true nature magically appears before you.

There are many reasons to keep an altar. You may wish to honor your ancestors. This can be as simple as keeping a photograph of your deceased grandmother on your altar, or it can encompass symbols or pictures representing your ethnic or cultural heritage. It might even include a variety of mythopoetic ancestors, such as goddesses or folk heroines. Imagine that you can trace your heritage back to the beginning of time— a world of possible ancestors unfolds before you. Honoring the elders is a vital concern in modern life, for all of us stand on many shoulders, yet today's youth-oriented society chooses to ignore this debt to those who went before us. Keeping an altar as a symbol of your homage is a potent way to connect with the wise ones of old.

A practical incentive for keeping an altar is its ability to provide a place for simple ceremonies. You may fear that an altar requires long meditations or elaborate rites to justify the effort put into creating it in the first place. This is definitively untrue. Once assembled the altar provides a setting for easy rituals such as lighting a candle while you practice a breathing meditation each morning, or arranging a bouquet of fragrant flowers and inhaling their calming aroma at bedtime. An altar helps you to quickly focus on the spirituality inherent in common things, such as the flicker of a candle flame or the heady scent of freshly picked lilacs.

Outdoor altars celebrate nature and offer you the healing power of the wild. A nature altar provides the privacy of the wilderness, the peace of a backyard garden, or the inspiration of the seashore. Spending a little time at an outdoor altar reminds you that you are not alienated from the rhythms of nature, for you are composed of earth (flesh), air (breath), water (blood), and fire (energy).

If you are a person in the arts, whether a dabbler or a professional, an altar dedicated to creativity will enhance your work. Place your altar in the room where you draw or paint or sculpt, or create an altar using your finished drawing, painting, or sculpture as the centerpiece. Use your altar as your writing table, or dance before your altar, or recite poetry to your altar, or play an instrument for your altar. Whatever your artistic passion, an altar dedicated to that which fires you creatively acts as a muse to continuously inspire you.

Acknowledge the special nature of your daily life with your altar. Whether you enjoy cooking, taking a bath, doing yoga, or gardening, include a symbol of the activity

The altar bridges the gap between a woman and her wisdom; between a woman and her inner world; between a woman and her path in life.

on your altar: a bowl of uncooked grain, a decorative glass bottle of bath oil, a picture of someone practicing yoga, fresh flowers from your garden.

A dream altar helps you gather your dreams, look at them clearly, and learn from them. Sit at your altar each morning as you scribble in a dream journal. Draw a picture of the dominant image in one of your dreams. Then give the journal a place of honor on your altar. This will stimulate the deep mind to produce more vivid dreams. Use a dream pillow to enhance your dreams.[1] A dream pillow is a small pillow filled with six herbs known to encourage dreams: mugwort, rose, lavender, hops, rosemary, and chamomile. Leave the pillow on or beside your altar during the day and tuck it under your bed pillow at night to bring good dreams and soothe away bad ones.

3

the realm of possibility:
what kind of altar?

Which kind of altar will you make? Permanent or temporary? Seasonal or "change at whim"? Indoor or outdoor? We will discuss the question of theme in more detail in the next chapter, so for now let's focus on the different types of altars. The choices are many.

A permanent altar requires less care than a temporary one because once it's set up your only tasks are dusting it, washing the altar cloth occasionally, and replacing the candle stubs with fresh tapers. The downside of a permanent altar is its tendency to blend in with the wallpaper and therefore not call to you as strongly as an altar which is changed according to the calendar, season, or whenever the mood strikes.

Halfway between a permanent altar and a "change at whim" altar lies the temporary altar. Seasonal altars are common temporary altars and lend themselves to many creative possibilities. A lunar altar can be changed weekly to reflect the four stages of the moon's cycle (dark, waxing crescent, full, and waning crescent). Or, the lunar altar can be changed monthly at the full moon, the name of that particular moon revealing the theme—such as the Corn Moon of August or the Long Night Moon of December.[2] Another path might be a solar altar which honors the eight Earth Holidays: Winter Solstice, Candlemas, Spring Equinox, May Day, the Summer Solstice, Lammas, Autumn Equinox, and Halloween.[3]

On a different note, if you're an artist, writer, poet, or dancer, you may want to create a "change at whim" altar to your particular art. Change this altar several times over the course of your creative project:

the original altar calls upon your muse to inspire the project

the first change honors the beginning of the project

the next change helps sustain you as the project moves through periods of stagnation

the third change observes the process of completing the project

the last change celebrates the project's conclusion

Nature abounds with places to create seasonal outdoor altars. For example, planting a ring of crocus bulbs in the fall will create a spring altar. Another altar could be a flat rock in a secluded spot, which you decorate with flowers, dried herbs and grasses, or crystals and feathers. Within your backyard garden, make an altar of whichever patch of earth is currently in bloom. Whether a bush or flowering tree, flowerbed or rock garden—this patch becomes the central visual stimulus for your meditation each day. Most "found" altars are outdoor altars: the tree stump hollowed out to make a perfect niche for a bouquet of wildflowers, or a large rock overlooking the ocean that forms a perfect ledge, beckoning you to come, sit awhile and meditate on the sight, smell, and sound of the ocean.

As your altar practice progresses, you may keep a number of different altars simultaneously. Perhaps a seasonal garden altar outside, a permanent altar to your deceased grandmother in the master bedroom, and a temporary altar in your meditation room dedicated to the four elements and their complementary season: air for spring, fire for summer, water for fall, and earth for winter. If you add things to your altar over time, you may reach a point when it looks cluttered. At this point, consider starting fresh. If you no longer see your altar when you enter a room, it probably needs to be changed so it will grab your awareness again.

Nature abounds with places to create seasonal outdoor altars.

4 life themes:
*how to create
a personal altar*

In the previous chapter, we considered the different types of altars: permanent, season-al, and "change at whim." We also discussed the difference between indoor and outdoor altars. In this chapter, we learn how to further develop our altars according to theme. If you are unsure where to begin, set aside some "quiet time" and contemplate any of the following thought-provoking questions:

"What am I thankful for?"

"What gives me peace?"

"What healing or blessing do I need?"

"What inspires me?"

"What is magical in my life?"

"What makes me feel special?"

"What in my life excites me, gets my juices flowing, makes me feel alive?"

Jot down your answers. The questions focus you on both the difficulties and the blessings in your life. The answers become the fertile soil from which spring the themes for your personal altars.

The summary section in the back of this book lists several possible themes for your altar. Part of that list includes:

Honor Mother Nature

Connect with the energy of wind, fire, earth, or water

Pay homage to a totem animal or a deceased pet

Gather healing energies for yourself or another

Offer thanks

Prepare for a difficult task

Bring good luck

Connect with the muse of creativity

Gather your dreams

Pay homage to the holiness of daily life

Any of these—or one of your own—is a perfect altar theme.

If you are a meditation teacher you may want to create an altar for each class. You might ask the other meditators to bring something different each week to symbolize whatever they wish to meditate on. During the class the altar is the visual focal point. At the end of class the altar is dismantled and people bring new objects the following week, so over time the altar represents the changing needs and concerns of the group.

Emotions such as joy, sorrow, anger, pain, love, and loss can be the focus of an altar. During the first year of mourning following the death of a loved one, you may integrate a snapshot of the deceased into the various altars you create. This inclusion helps you see the changes in the mourning process over the course of the year. Or you may focus on the joy of a new grandchild with pictures of her changing looks chronicling her first year on Earth.

Sometimes the theme for your altar will come to you in an unexpected way. For example, you come across a blue jay's feather in your back yard. You instinctively pick it up and turn it over in your hand. The feather begins a flow of thought. The color reminds you of a startling blue place mat tucked away in the linen drawer. You remember a gorgeous picture of a bird in flight from a nature magazine. The bird was photographed against a dawn sky just before sunrise. You become aware that yellow candles will mimic the sun's glow and accent the yellows in the picture. Before you realize it, you've found the theme, the colors, the centerpiece—all inspired by a blue jay's feather, which you now lay in a place of honor in the center of your altar.

Once you choose the intention for your altar, select a place where you can set it up. Remember, an altar can be created anywhere, outdoors or indoors. Any location that makes you feel special, peaceful, powerful, or appreciative is the perfect spot for an altar. Once you make a place special through the creation of an altar, you begin to respond to that place with a certain reverence. The altar absorbs and retains some of this reverential energy and so, over time, you become aware of the interplay of energy between you, the altar-maker, and your creation, the altar.

You have a theme and you've chosen a place. The question is now, "What do you place on your altar?" The answer is, "Anything you please!" When choosing objects for your altar, select those that revolve around your theme.

If you find inspiration in nature, consider which of the four elements you feel the most affinity toward and dedicate your altar to that element. Choose flags, fans, or bird

An altar is a place where you give attention to objects and people and places that matter to you.

feathers to represent air, and bowls of spring water, seashells, or essence oils to symbolize water. Gems, stones, crystals, potting soil, plants, and flowers for earth; candles, incense, pictures of flames or drawings of the sun for fire. Any or all of the four elements can be represented on your nature altar, whether it be indoors or out. If you wish to represent all four elements on your indoor nature altar, you might include a candle for fire, a paper fan for air, flowers for earth, and a bowl of water.

Another aspect of nature is the animal kingdom. You might decorate your altar with a drawing of your totem animal (a helping spirit that comes to you in your dreams or reveries in the form of an animal), a photo of your favorite wild animal, or a picture of a pet. This altar space is created to honor these beings that are in sync with the natural forces of the universe in a way we can only hope to emulate. By creating this altar you are establishing a connection to a nature-centered view of the world.

Perhaps your theme centers on your desire to spend more time at the ocean. To mirror this need, choose objects that reflect your love of the sea: a watercolor of the ocean, a bowl of beach sand, a dried starfish, and a snapshot of you frolicking in the ocean. These visual representations of your desire to visit the ocean will help you focus on that desire when you sit before your ocean altar.

The beach is the perfect setting for a temporary outdoor altar. Simply take a pail, fill it with sand, place a circle of sea-washed beach stones on the sand, and stick a sea gull feather into the center of the circle. In this way you have created a space apart which honors sky (feather), sea (beach stones), and earth (sand).

Consider creating an altar to pay tribute to the private self hidden deep within the psyche. For this type of altar choose objects that symbolize disparate parts of your

inner self. An altar honoring your many selves emanates a wild beauty, a terrible truth, an awesome power. The altar becomes a stage upon which the inner and outer selves merge, creating a wholeness that is truly healing.

Relax and trust the altar-making process. Know that various objects such as scarves for altar cloths, statues, pictures, candles, and candleholders will find their way to you. Objects you find around the house, in the yard, or in the shed will suddenly appear in a different light as you become more in tune with the art of altar creation. Altar objects are sacred because you consider them special—that is the only criterion.

The ritual aspect of altars need not be an integral part of altar making. You may be content to create a corner of beauty, or a shrine to your current passion, or a space that displays your creative work. Without ever "doing" anything at the altar, your particular altar arrangement will enhance your creativity, or feed your current passion, or increase your appreciation of beauty. Altars, even without the ritual aspect, have a deep effect on the mind because you've taken the time and energy to set something apart. This fact says to the mind, "Pay attention. What stands on my altar holds special meaning for me!" The shapes, colors, and symbols of an altar can bring you serenity at the end of a busy day, provide a pattern of connection to the changing seasons, and afford you strength when you feel discouraged—all without ever lighting a single candle. Your altar evokes a certain state of mind whenever you behold it. It is sufficient unto itself.

5

spiritual journey:
what to do at your altar

You create an altar when you draw together meaningful symbols in order to focus attention on something significant in your life. The act of working with the energies of these symbolic objects creates ritual. An altar becomes a surface on which ceremonies or active meditations are performed in order to stimulate a fuller awareness of the special intent of your altar. These rituals or rites may be taken from books, created from your imagination, or inspired by rituals you've seen in church, at meditation classes, or in expressive therapy groups. Each ritual is an intimate dance with your essential self through which you can articulate your struggles, your strengths, and your oneness with nature, as well as your unity with the important people in your life.

To complete the ritual ground the energy by bowing to the altar, or placing your hands on the floor in front of the altar. Grounding symbolizes the end of the ritual and signals the mind to return to an ordinary state of awareness as you re-enter daily life. If you plan to do ritual at your altar, assemble it in a quiet space where you'll not be interrupted. Ritual includes two aspects: intention and attention. Your intention is displayed on your altar, but the type of attention paid to this intention requires a shift in consciousness in order to be thought of as ritual. This deepening occurs naturally whenever you concentrate, contemplate, meditate, or create. Ritual brings you deep within your mind to a place where changes in your attitude occur. From these attitudinal shifts come the changes in your outer life. Ritual actions communicate with the deep mind using a language of symbols. Actions do speak louder than words when bringing a message to the unconscious, the realm where change originates. Altars created for their own sake help you reconnect with the universal life force. Rituals performed at the altars help you use that life energy to create change.

In the first chapter, we discussed a spring altar comprised of water, a hyacinth, and a hand-crafted clay ladle. You could perform a simple ceremony each morning by dipping the ladle into the water and then pouring that water over the hyacinth. This ritual combines the loving memory of your grandmother (represented by the hyacinth) with the renewing qualities of the water and the earthy, artistic character of the clay.

In chapter 4, we considered making an altar based on a desire to spend more time at the ocean. As ritual, sit before this altar every day. The ritual of sitting honors the desire, which in turn energizes your intention. This fresh energy spills forth in your conversations during the course of your day; you find yourself mentioning your desire to spend time at the ocean to more and more people, thereby increasing your chances of connecting with a solution to the dilemma. The solution could take many forms: Perhaps a friend will rent a beach house and ask you to share it for a summer. Maybe you'll be offered a new job near the ocean. Maybe you'll discover an affordable home in a seaside community. In some way, the sea will become a more integral part of your life. The ritual makes it all possible.

When performing any ritual,
end with a thank-you to your
deeper self, a higher power,
Mother Nature, or whatever
you feel is greater than you.

Remember our altar paying tribute to our hidden, private selves? A brief ceremony could be performed each morning to honor our wholeness. Begin by lighting a candle and in a slow, ceremonious way, bow to the altar three times. Do not close your eyes but instead take in all the symbols of your hidden self that are displayed on the altar. Then stand before the altar for a full five minutes contemplating this inner self. Extinguish the candle and go forth into the day knowing a more integrated you faces the world.

Use an altar to enhance your sensuality. You need not find a special place for this altar. Your dressing table or bureau top will do nicely. Remove everything from the space you've chosen, except the mirror. Place a couple of candles on this altar and contemplate a sensual look that you'd like to experiment with this evening.

Choose sensuous, mysterious, or magical background music. On the altar place a dish of water, a fragrant flower, face make-up, body glitter , hairbrush, comb, jewelry, hair ornaments—anything that makes you feel exotic, elegant, or alluring (depending on which look you are trying to create).

The ritual begins with lighting the candles (extinguish all electric lights) and closing your eyes. As you sit before the mirror listening to the music, picture yourself as Cleopatra, for example. See her doing her hair and make-up. What would she wear? How would she carry herself? Create a whole scene. Let this reverie go on until the imagery fades. Open your eyes and, by candlelight, anoint yourself as the woman you've daydreamed into existence. Take the flower, dip it in the water, and anoint your face and body. This rite of purification (cleansing the surface mind of doubt and worry concerning your sensuality) allows you to deepen, becoming the woman of amazing

beauty and grace that you birthed in your guided imagery. This ritual blessing of the body can also be performed with the smoke from a stick of incense, or using daubs of essence oil or perfume.

Now begin doing your hair and make-up in some creative fashion. For instance, you may have seen yourself as the Lady of the Wild Things, so you might twist ivy into your hair and choose earth tones for your make-up, transforming yourself into the queen of nature. This altar ritual allows you to take time to appreciate your innate beauty, while exploring your sensuous, magical self.

A totally different kind of altar, the kitchen altar, pays homage to the holiness of daily life. Gather the vegetables and flowers from your field and garden in the early morning. Thank the land for its yield while you wash the fruits and vegetables and place the flowers in water. Then display the harvest in a corner of your kitchen on a tabletop, sideboard, or windowsill. Light a candle on this altar (you might also include a kitchen goddess[4] or kitchen witch in amongst the crops), and ask a blessing on the food and flowers that will grace your supper table. If you wish to draw upon the inherent energy of this altar you could write a petition for you or a family member while the candle remains lit. Using a wineglass or goblet, drink a toast (water, wine, or juice) to Mother Nature, asking her to grant your request. Leave the written petition on the altar and extinguish the candle. During the course of your day, the kitchen altar will excite your senses with the colors, shapes, and scents of nature's bounty.

As the above examples illustrate, rituals are as elaborate—or simple—as you wish. Sometimes a simple morning or evening ceremony performed daily or weekly will do.

Other times, you might want to make a night of your ritual. If you are new to ritual practice, keep in mind that these rites are performed to offer an avenue of expression to the deeper self and, therefore, can be seen as active prayer or meditation in motion. The rest of this chapter explains several different directions you may follow when designing your own ritual.

You needn't be able to sing to perform ceremonies of the voice. Try humming one droning note, or reading aloud a few lines from a favorite poem, or reciting a mantra for three to five minutes. Ceremonies of the voice are about making sounds, any sounds. A wonderful way to begin is to sing or chant the vowels, allowing the vowel sounds to open the throat, empty the lungs, and express the heart.

If you are a poet, a vowel-chanting exercise could begin a ritual in which you read one of your poems aloud. Consider the dual acts of loosening your voice and reading the poem as an invocation to your muse. This short ceremony could begin with lighting a candle and conclude with meditatively extinguishing it with a candle snuffer. Before snuffing the candle, leave a copy of your poem on the altar. Perform this ritual for many reasons: to assuage stage fright before a public reading, to light the fires of inspiration before a rewrite, to offer thanks for the publication of the poem, to celebrate concluding a volume of your poems, to rejoice as you break through a period of writer's block.

You don't need to use your voice in every ritual. You may be an artist who wishes to silently connect with your source of inspiration. Place a picture or symbol of that which inspires you on your altar: the sea, the mountains, the Goddess, the muse, a favorite artist, an historical figure, a fictional character, an animal, or a bird. Light a stick of incense. While it burns, softly gaze at the picture. As you open your mind and heart to inspiration, feel that your creative juices are fed by this act of re-dedication.

Whether you use tarot or angel cards, a dowsing rod, a crystal ball, or another tool, any act of divination can be made ceremonial by first lighting a candle on your altar and performing a simple ritual with a bowl of water.[5] Close your eyes and place both hands into the bowl of clear, fresh water. Say to yourself,

The submerging of my hands represents the journey I am about to take. During this reading I will travel beneath the surface of the conscious mind to the watery realm of the unconscious.

Remove your hands and dry them thoroughly on a clean towel before you begin. Remember that you are not foretelling the future but rather tuning into the hidden (unconscious) aspects of the "here and now." The oracle illuminates the unconscious anxieties, needs, and desires that are secretly motivating you. Once you are aware of these motivations, you can choose to ignore or integrate this information about the deeper forces shaping the present. Since the future grows out of the present, you can alter it by assimilating this new view of your present life. The oracle can help you decide which direction to take at any given moment, but it cannot create the future for you—that choice remains yours.

Rituals of the heart involve our emotions on an interpersonal level and our devotional feelings toward the Divine (whether God, Goddess, the alpha state, the unconscious mind, a saint, an angel, a holy site, the sacredness of Earth, a spirit guide, or simply the powers that be). To perform a simple ritual of the heart, wear an article of red clothing (scarf, skirt, shawl, sweater) to represent the fire of your passion. Sit before two lit, red tapers and create a red heart in some imaginative way. Make your heart from red Play-Doh, twine red flowers around a heart-shaped wreath frame, cut it out from red foil paper, shape it from red candy sprinkles, fill a heart-shaped basket with red flowers, or fill a heart-shaped cake pan with red sand. Throughout the process, repeat this mantra: "I'm forming my heart from love." Then place the heart on your altar to display and affirm your loving nature.

Rites of music include listening to or creating music, or a combination of the two. The music can be as simple as ringing a bell, shaking a wind chime, or rattling a tambourine. Play a recording of a favorite piece of music in the background, if the idea of making music intimidates you. If you are a novice at music making, percussion instruments are a good place to start. Sit before your altar in a room lit only by candles (this will add a magical element to the ritual) and meditatively look at your drum or rattle or rain stick to create a connection between you and it. Then close your eyes and slowly run your hands over the instrument. Open your eyes and experiment with different sounds you make on your instrument. Begin drumming (or rattling) in sync with the background music. Shadow dance with your instrument to end the ritual. While facing a blank wall in the candlelight, move to the beat while lifting your drum overhead, then reaching down to the floor, then stretch it out to the side. Loosen up and feel free to experiment with both sound and movement. End by ceremoniously placing your instrument on or near your altar.

Perfuming the air becomes a simple ceremony if you sit at your altar and:

crush herbs using mortar and pestle

arrange fragrant flowers in a vase

braid sweet grass

burn incense or scented candles or sage

A more elaborate ceremony might include dipping a sweet-smelling flower in a small bowl of water and anointing your body with the water. The act of moving the flower through the air allows the scent to permeate your altar, your room, and yourself.

Some rites help you discover a link to your creativity. Decorate a mask with paints, stickers, sparkles, crayons—anything that represents creativity to you. The mask embodies your creative self. Before any creative activity, gaze at yourself for a full five minutes wearing the mask. This image is your creative self. Every time you wear the mask you cover up the external, superficial self and manifest a deeper, more authentic, creative part of your being. This ceremony creates a gulf between your normal consciousness and the expanded awareness needed for any creative endeavor and then signals a step into the creative realms. This ritual is not only for artists, it is for everyone. We are all creative people. We are all artists in some way, whether we create a special meal, a house, a child, or a garden. Look at your life. What is that you do with joy? That is your art, your creative contribution to the world!

The rites of writing are as varied as an author's imaginative meandering. Bless your work by placing it on your altar and waving a lit stick of incense over it. Each morning do a short imagery exercise in which you picture the work already published. Visualize your name in print on the full-color cover. If your work has been published, leave the book on the altar and each evening read a page or two aloud as an act of thanksgiving to the muse that inspired you. If you're suffering from writer's block, make a collage: Cut pictures from a magazine, selecting ones that represent the forces that are blocking you. Sit at your altar and glue the pictures to a piece of poster-board. Leave the collage on your altar for a week. At the end of that time, cut up the collage and burn it piece-by-piece in a fireproof container on your altar. This ritual may well jog your unconscious mind, releasing material to be worked on once again.

When you feel that the good things in life are passing you by, you need a ritual to open yourself to abundance. The ritual centers on assuming some responsibility for this state of affairs and working with it. To begin, sit at your altar with ten ribbons, each about one inch wide, three feet long, and in a different color. Each ribbon represents one of ten "goodies" you wish were part of your life: "I wish I had more free time." "I wish I had more money." "I wish I had a lover." Tie a knot in each ribbon to represent your self-pity. Set up an ironing board in front of the altar. Untie each knotted ribbon and iron it smooth while saying, "Everything opens when I open me." Let the ironing of each ribbon symbolize transforming the energy in each knot of self-pity into an offering of thanksgiving for the blessings already present in your life. Now place the freshly ironed ribbons on your altar, one at a time, naming aloud something in your life for

which you are thankful. Leave the ribbons on the altar for a week to remind you that counting your blessings helps you untangle yourself from self-pity. Now unknotted, you are open to receive other blessings that perhaps passed you by. After all, the open hand receives more manna from heaven than the closed fist. You must first be in a receptive state before blessings can reach you. Open your hand, open your heart, iron your ribbons.

6
seasonal offerings:
winter, spring, summer
and autumn altars

Traditionally these would remain in place for three months each, but you might consider creating two altars for each season, since the early days of each season often contain much of the previous season's weather.

Winter

winter moon slides
between bits of flung foil
shooting-stars

January, 1998

The season of bare branches and early nightfall may tempt you to ask, "Is there anything about this season worth celebrating?" In addition to skiing, snowmen, and sleigh rides, there's the glimmering sunlight on freshly fallen snow, the clarity of winter air, and the abundance of starglow and moonlight on long nights. As well as the opportunity to witness the sunrise each morning, since the sun peeks up around 7 A.M., a full two hours later than it rises in summer months. From late December through February your winter altar could be dedicated to watching the sun rise!

A sunrise altar beckons you to get up before the sun so you can await its glowing arrival. Since sun symbolizes warmth and energy, this altar embodies your bulwark against the cold and lethargy of winter months. Each time you look at it during the course of your day, you are reminded of the sun's glorious face, even if the outdoor world is suffering the bluster and blow of a snowstorm. Light a few candles on your altar as you wait out the storm!

To create the winter altar, position a table under an east-facing window. Gather objects that reflect the beauty of a winter morning: a snowy white tablecloth, a blue glass bowl (the color of a clear winter sky), and gold candles (sun-colored), for example. Each morning, fill the bowl anew with fresh spring water.

For the ritual, perform a few rounds of the yoga pose called *Salute to the Sun*. Or try some Tai Chi. If these seem too foreign or strenuous, any bend-and-stretch

exercises done slowly, with attention to breathing deeply throughout the series, will work just as well. To complete the ritual, dip your hands into the bowl and splash your face three times with the spring water. Allow the water to run down your face as you lift your head to watch the rising sun. Feel the water and sunshine mingling to initiate you into the exhilarating clarity of a new day. The value of this ritual lies in its ability to stave off winter lethargy, for anyone who watches the sunrise is blessed with the energy of first light.

Spring

snow-broken

flowering branches

empty flute

April 1997

The aliveness of early spring is worth celebrating after the chill and isolation of winter. For months the earth has lain dormant in a suspended state of active waiting, in anticipation of the gradual warming that earmarks late March and all of April. Winter's stranglehold on the land is loosening. Colors, sounds, and scents slowly return. The red winged blackbird is heard once more. Streams gurgle, overflowing with snowmelt. The plump, silver-velvet catkins of the pussywillows are visible, as are the bright green, curled tops of the fiddlehead ferns.

An outdoor altar is the perfect way to honor the increased light and milder temperatures that foster spring's return. Plan this altar in the fall by planting a circle of bulbs in your yard. Crocus, hyacinth, daffodils, or tulips will work well. Make the circle about six feet in diameter. Begin your ritual at the first glimpse of brilliant green shoots beginning to peek through the brown earth. The absence of winter's penetrating winds and bitter cold makes it feasible to perform this ritual daily.

Use the area within the circle as your altar surface. Each day, stand in the center of the circle. Begin by examining the minute, day-to-day changes taking place in the shoots as they slowly begin to reveal tight buds tucked within their green leaves. Over time the buds open to glorious blossoms that brighten the yard with stunning colors.

Your ritual is a simple ceremony: Raise your arms to the sky. Feel the wind puffing through your hair and gaze up at the clear, blue expanse. Breathe deeply. With each in-breath imagine that you are pulling the color of the sky and the warmth of the sun into your being. As you exhale, connect with the burgeoning impulse within the soil beneath your feet. Squat down, place both hands on Mother Earth, and thank her for yet another glorious spring.

It is also wise to create an indoor altar, since spring showers may interrupt your altar practice. Use bright yellow candles to symbolize the spring sun and a blue table cloth to represent the sky. Keep a bouquet of fresh flowers on the altar to embody the greenery and fragrance of spring.

Summer

molten sun

at flower's center

wild river

June, 1997

Summer's the season for leaving behind all your cares and spending some time at the beach, maybe even renting a cottage at the shore for your vacation. Whether you are one of the fortunate who spend your whole summer by the sea or someone who gets away for an occasional day at the beach, the ocean provides an opportunity to discover a "found" altar. Bring nothing with you for this altar except a small bouquet of flowers. Choose a time of day when the beach will be deserted or almost empty. Begin your solitary walk by seeing the entire stretch of beach as your altar. Your ritual is a long, barefoot walk in the sand at water's edge. Notice how the tempo of your steps mimics the rhythms of the sea, while your deep breathing connects you to the ocean breeze. The decoration for the beach altar is provided anew each day. The sea offers up beach stones, seaweed, driftwood, shells, and the occasional starfish. Music for this ritual is provided by the roar and hush of the ocean, the slap of the waves, the shriek of a gull.

At the end of your walk cast the flowers, one-by-one, onto the tide, naming a specific blessing as you throw each blossom to the sea. Take your time with this ritual. Watch each flower bob in the ocean as you focus on your grateful feelings for that particular blessing. Expressing gratitude opens the heart and creates channels through which more blessing can reach you. Folks who are often heard lamenting, "Nothing good ever comes my way!" are probably not appreciative of the blessings life has already showered upon them.

To end this ritual, draw in the wet sand a word or phrase or symbol that represents a wish. Know that the magic of your expressed gratitude will greatly enhance the chances of your wish coming true.

Autumn

Autumn's Fruit

I pick you
my pagan pomegranate
you the purplish apple
of Eve's delight

Stained fingers deep
in your red flesh
I choose one seed from
your multitude of young

on my tongue the taste of
Eden

November, 1997

Rather than seeing fall as yielding only apples, squash, pumpkins, pomegranates, bittersweet, chrysanthemums and the like, you may, with the help of an altar, honor the spiritual lesson inherent in this season.

Autumn can seem sad. The gloriously-colored leaves are trampled under foot, the fields are bare, the daylight is decreasing, and death seems to reign as you prepare to face the long white of winter. Autumn appears to be a brilliant burst of color that is all too fleeting!

To prepare your autumn altar, gather a few leaves and paint them with clear nail polish to preserve the vibrancy of their colors. Spread the leaves on a burgundy altar cloth and notice the colors glow against the dark fabric. Light two orange candles and meditate on the life of the leaves. They began as chartreuse buds in the early spring, then grew large enough to offer welcome shade during the summer months. Now that they've shared their glorious hues, the leaves await an ignominious death as they are raked into piles and heaped upon barren gardens.

But consider the fact that nothing in nature dies. Energy is released and transformed. But these leaves do seem to be dying, don't they? There is the appearance of death as one form is discarded and another taken on, but the energy moves in an unbroken circle through all the seasons of the year. Over time the leaves change into warm compost that protects the garden in winter and nourishes it in the form of rich soil come springtime. The same energy that enlivened the leaves as they clung to their branches is presently transforming them into mulch. It takes the whole winter for this transmutation to occur. Even during winter, a season that to all outward appearances looks dead, the eternal life-giving energy of nature flows continuously.

To perform an autumn ritual, move the leaves to one side and place two bowls on the altar: one with potting soil in it, the other containing sparkly gold confetti. Once a week, sit at the altar and contemplate an aspect of your life that you consider an ending, a cessation, a death. Look at it from every angle until you discover the harvest-gift intrinsic to this dying process. Take a handful of confetti and mix it into the soil, using your fingers. Say, "I give thanks for the harvest of my life. I'm especially thankful for the hidden blessings that disguise themselves as burdens. In the same way that the warmth from the dying leaves benefits my garden, the losses in my life enrich the compost of my experience. May the glitter of this confetti represent the vital spark of the life energies as it transforms the small deaths in my life into gifts of the harvest."

Extinguish the candles and place the leaves back where they were before. Leave the clear glass bowl of sparkly soil in the center to remind you of autumn's lesson.

7
soul purpose:
special intention altars

Any altar dedicated to a specific intention has an open-ended timeline, unlike seasonal altars that are set up for approximately three months. Special intention altars remain in place until there's a shift in your internal awareness causing you to no longer need to focus on this intention, or until there's been an external change in the situation that brought about the creation of this altar initially.

Prayer Flag Altar

hymn

response-heart
beats that sound
tunes the chosen melody
of beseech-magic

beneath the chant
words gain-ride the rhythm
lift the music into
sung prayer

May, 2001

This altar explores the concept that worry can be turned inside out into healing energy. Consider a friend or family member who is currently in crisis. You are deeply concerned for her, yet feel powerless to help. Her difficulties preoccupy your thoughts not only during your spare time, but also while you ought to be working. Creating a prayer flag altar can turn your helplessness into healing by continually reminding you that life is in a constant state of flux—given time, this too shall pass.

Find a flowing, brightly colored scarf and hang it in a breezy spot: a tree branch, a clothesline, a tall fence post, a corner of your deck, or a porch railing. It needs to be high enough to catch the wind, yet low enough for you to easily reach it. Put a small outdoor table under the flag. In the center, place a small container of flowers with a lantern on either side (or candles in tall glass containers). Fill a small pail with tap water or water from a lake, stream, or spring, if you are fortunate enough to have any such body of water nearby. At this point you've assembled a symbol for each of the four elements, and you're ready to begin the ritual you'll perform daily.

Light the lanterns. Untie the scarf and consecrate it with fire by holding it over the lanterns, then spritz it with water, touch it to the soil beneath the flowers, and hold it aloft to catch the breeze. Now that wind, water, earth, and fire have lent their intrinsic energies to the scarf, nature's blessings have transformed it into a prayer flag. Close your eyes. Contemplate the powers of these four natural forces of the universe. Hold your flag aloft to catch the breeze. As you listen to the flap and flutter of your prayer flag, imagine waves of light moving from the flag to your friend or loved one, carrying with it your heartfelt blessings for a speedy end to the crisis. Say mentally or aloud,

This colorful flag flies night and day. When the breeze blows

may healing light wing its way to my friend, _____.

Thanks be to the power of the wind!

Open your eyes and tie the prayer flag high in the breeze. Extinguish the candles. Know in your heart that in the coming days each time you catch a glimpse of the flag flying against the sky, you'll be reminded to transform the burden of your worry into the blessing of healing thoughts. Obsessive, negative thinking contains great amounts of psychic energy. Rather than attempting to suppress this thinking by telling yourself to "stop worrying!" be grateful for the amount of energy contained in your worrisome thoughts and use this energy to send forth a positive message. It takes but a shift in focus to allow your vision of a situation to undergo a radical change. The daily altar ceremony will strengthen your resolve to focus on the positive and help you recall that you have an ally in nature—the wind that carries light to your friend or loved one. The prayer flag altar becomes a stage upon which a crisis can become a healing.

The Artist's Altar

muse

the long arms

of your light

embrace me

still

February, 1998

Artists are natural altar makers! Whether you paint, dance, sing, play an instrument, write, act, or draw, an altar enhances your creativity. Altars are places set aside as sacred space. However, any space where you practice your art becomes sacred by virtue of the nature of the energy that flows there, for artistic creations arise from the same deep wellspring of the unconscious mind as religious ceremony. Religious ritual can be viewed as an art form just as artistic activity can be seen as a form of prayer. Prayer, meditation, and contemplation all require a shift in consciousness. In addition, art is created from a similar state of expanded awareness, one in which you express your creativity from a deeper aspect of yourself.

Any place in which you create art becomes sacred because at those artistic moments you are in sync with the primordial forces that fire nature's cycles of creation, preservation, destruction, and new creation. Looking at the origins of art in this light allows you to view all art spaces as altars: the writing desk, the floor where you practice dance, the easel that holds your canvas, the stool you sit on to practice guitar.

In addition to these casual altars, set up an altar table in the corner of your studio or practice space. Begin by covering it with a cloth that is hand-woven or hand-painted, or that in some way connects you to artistic endeavor. On it put a bell, a candle, and anything that symbolizes your specific artistic genre. Begin each practice session with a short ceremony: ring the bell to signal to your mind that it's time to deepen, for a busy mind constantly intent on the superficial details of life has no room for the subliminal proddings that give rise to art. Then light a candle that will remain lit while you are busy creating. Before you leave the room, bow to your altar of creativity honoring the powers of inspiration and place any unfinished work (diagrams of steps for a new dance, a poem, song lyrics, musical compositions, or a short story) on the altar. This is a signal to your deeper mind to continue working on the unfinished piece, while you go forth to deal with your day job. Know that the next time you look at the unfinished work, a flood of ideas will rise to the surface and your creative energies will flow.

Every artist experiences droughts. These can be viewed as periods of active waiting, natural rest periods in the creative cycle. But if you feel this dormancy has gone on far too long, your altar can help end this arid period. To liven up your artistic energies, try rearranging the objects on your altar. If that doesn't solve the problem, change the altar completely. Since your altar symbolizes your artistic efforts, creating a new altar can stimulate your mind to make a fresh start. Remember the altar is the meeting place for various energies: personal and universal, conscious and unconscious, mundane and creative. Changing the altar stimulates these collected energies, bringing the magic of the unexpected into your artistic endeavors.

An Altar for Difficult Times

under snow

crocuses open

fire-harvest

April, 1997

Are you living in dread of an event due to take place in the near future? Whether your fear centers on a theatrical performance, a business presentation at an important meeting, an emotional conflict with a friend, or asking for a raise, creating an altar to confront your apprehension will benefit you greatly.

The simple act of choosing to make such an altar is a powerful statement, since many people do not have the courage to face difficulty head on, preferring endless worry to taking action. If you choose to assemble an altar dedicated to facing a specific fear, you'll be amazed at the altar's ability to provide the sustenance you need. The disagreeable task will be no less onerous, but the altar will become your ally in transforming anxiety into confidence.

Begin by putting a table by a window that gets ample sun, as sunlight is a source of positive energy. Use a piece of brightly colored fabric for the altar cloth. Place a freestanding mirror at the center of the altar. A candle and a bell (wind chimes, jingle bells, cow bell, or dinner bell) sit on opposite sides of the mirror. Next find some object (it must be small enough to fit in your hand) that represents you at your most powerful. It might be a mask, a piece of statuary, a painting, a photo, a piece of jewelry—something that speaks to you of your intrinsic worth. This becomes your touchstone. Place it at the center of the altar.

Light the candle. Take the touchstone in your hand and sit quietly, absorbing the strength and genuineness emanating from it. Look in the mirror and say aloud or mentally:

I am powerful

I am strong

Let this touchstone

Carry me along.

Do this mantra for a few minutes then sit in silence, letting the power of the words sink into your consciousness.

Everyone is blessed with the inner resources of courage and self-respect. This altar enshrines these powerful qualities and brings them to the forefront of your awareness, thus making them more accessible to you in your time of need. With the mantra you rev up the energy of your inner strength and simultaneously combat the negativity of "I don't want to! I can't! I'm scared!" phrases that pop into your mind every time you think of your upcoming encounter. The altar stands as a reminder that the day you are dreading will be an opportunity, not a showdown; a challenge, not a humiliation.

As you leave your house to face this challenge, take the touchstone with you—in your pocket, purse, or briefcase. Though it is wise to remember that the courage to face your fears comes from the deepest recesses of your own being, not from your touchstone, it is nonetheless comforting to have it with you.

Everyone is afraid of something. This "difficult times" altar lets you address your uneasiness, rather than permit your anxiety to make you timid when you need to be strong.

8

ceremony and tradition:
special occasion altars

The special occasion altar usually remains in place for a few hours while the ceremony or celebration takes place and is dismantled immediately thereafter. However, the travel altar can remain in place for the duration of your stay, and the mourning altar could become a permanent tribute to the deceased, so there are no specific timelines for this type of altar.

Birthday Altar

ocean

I am a field washed by the sea
my painted body   my glistening flesh
I am a field   wash of the sea
my driftwood bones slip through the net

I am a field swirled by the sea
my hair in the breeze   wind over grass

I am a field   swirl of the sea

a dancing breath on the back of my neck

I am a field rinsed by the sea

pull of my muscles   pulse of the beach

I am a field   rinse of the sea

heave of the ocean   sand on my breast

I am a field soaked by the sea

murmur of waves   tide at full stretch

I am a field   soak of the sea

smell of the earth   wide-open   wet

April, 1995

Begin your birthday morning with the creation of an altar to celebrate you! Start with a white altar cloth (a tablecloth, napkin, sheet, pillowcase, fabric remnant, or place mat). On the altar, place a bowl of spring water and three floating candles (one for each wish you'll make). Next to the candles, place paper and pen and a bowl of fresh flower petals. Buy a few flowers at the local market or pick some from your garden and keep them in water until just prior to the ritual. Pull off the petals and place them on the altar in a decorative container.

Complete the altar arrangement by choosing a different symbolic object for each decade of your life. For example, you might select a butterfly for the playful innocence of your first ten years, a jeweled bird for the beauty and flightiness of being a teen, a turtle for a decade that moved slowly, glue for one in which you felt stuck in a rut, a snake for a transformative decade, a sparkler for the fireworks of an exciting decade. These symbols represent your life thus far. Place these symbols around the base of the water bowl.

Contemplate three wishes for the coming year. Float the candles on the water's surface and, as you light each one, speak your wish out loud. Then float the petals on the water. As you drop each petal onto the water say:

I am the ocean

I am the sea

Everything opens

When I open me [6]

Repeat this until you feel your heart is open to receiving the blessings of your three wishes.

Let the candles burn down until they go out naturally. While watching the candles burn, visualize your wishes fulfilled in the here and now, imagine they are being granted in the present moment. Notice how you feel as your wishes come true.

To conclude your private birthday celebration, write down your wishes and leave the piece of paper on the altar. The altar may remain in place until the next morning or until the end of your birthday month. Or leave it in place for an entire year. Light a candle on the altar each morning to reenergize your wishes!

Public Monument Altar

outdoor shrine

beads coins flowers fruit

offered up to

thieves

April, 1999

If you are a city lover, chances are you can think of at least one outdoor monument or sculpture that never ceases to amaze you. You find this piece of public art inspirational because of its beauty or size, or because you admire the person it honors. Such is the case for me in Boston's Copley Square. At one end of the square sits a monument to Kahlil Gibran, the Lebanese poet-philosopher who spent the last years of his life helping the poor in the Mission Hill section of Boston. The inscription on his monument reads: "It was in my heart to help a little because I was helped much." This inspirational quote is barely noticed by the hoards rushing by each day.

However, you can call attention to any piece of outdoor art and, in so doing, make it into a public altar by buying a bouquet of flowers and placing them on or near the monument. In this way you are making public your personal attachment to this work of art. Once the flowers are in place, it's an interesting ritual to sit nearby and watch the reactions of passersby. Some notice the bunch of flowers and keep walking; some stop to admire the bouquet; some pause long enough to read the inscription. In this way you share some of your appreciation of the energy emanating from this work of art. Many folks who usually rush by see the breathtaking beauty of this monument only because you've made an altar of it through the simple addition of flowers. What may subliminally flash through the minds of the people passing is: "What gorgeous flowers—someone put them there deliberately. I wonder why? Let me take a minute to see what this is all about!" Your altar beckons to folks! In essence it is saying: "Come to your senses. Smell the flowers. Touch the sculpture. Be in the moment." In the midst of a big city, hell-bent on pursuing profit margins and bottom lines, you can help a little by sharing a public altar.

An Altar to Mourning

Celtic Tea

cup in hand

I step out on the porch

into the May dusk

capture the glimmer

of a waning crescent

in the brown sea

long ago

my Galway grandmother

chanted me to sleep

while the glider

squeaked accompaniment

may the moon

in its roundness

grant all

of your wishes

tonight

in this tiny cauldron

I sweeten the sliver

stir it into fullness

February, 2000

Few are ever prepared for the death of a loved one. Creating an altar dedicated to your deceased friend or relative can initiate healing in the midst of grief. The period of transition following a death overflows with emotion: shock, sadness, fear, guilt, and pain. An altar dedicated to mourning will offer you solace as you make the memory of the deceased as focal in the external world as it is in your interior life.

To begin, if you have a piece of furniture that belonged to the deceased, it would be fitting to use it: a cedar chest, small desk, table, bookcase, even a wooden kitchen chair will do. Any or all of the altar objects you choose could be selected from the belongings of the deceased, but this is by no means a necessity. The altar cloth might be a handkerchief, doily, or scarf. On it, place a photograph of the deceased, but only if this feels comforting to you. Add a candle and some incense and a porcelain plate with tulip bulbs arranged on it.

As you light the candle, invoke the name of the deceased, "_____, may this flame guide you on your journey to the afterlife." Close your eyes and envision your loved one. Then hold each bulb over the warmth of the candle flame and the smoke of the incense and say, " I consecrate these bulbs to your memory. I'll plant them at your gravesite in the autumn. Through the winter they'll lie buried next to you until, with the spring, they'll bloom, brimming over with life, bringing joy to all who see them—a perfect symbol of you and your *joie de vivre.*"

In our rushed society the value of the mourning altar is obvious: it gives you permission to take as long as you wish with the grieving process. You may keep the altar in place for a week, a month, a year, or as a permanent shrine. The altar becomes your personal connection to the deceased. Each time you light a candle and send warm thoughts to your loved one, you feel less helpless, for you are assisting her transition to the spirit world.

Travel Altar

house of gratitude

my heart sings

under a roof

of breath

December, 1997

Whether you are leaving behind all cares and ties to go on vacation, or packing for a business trip, a travel altar is a wonderful way to bring a personal/spiritual touch to a bland hotel room or rented beach house. Consider beforehand how much extra space you have in your luggage. Given airline limitations these days, you probably have very little.

A small candleholder, a votive candle, something aromatic (a lavender-scented eye mask, an herb-filled sachet, or a package of your favorite incense), and a small altar cloth (a linen handkerchief or an embroidered facecloth) will all fit easily in your suitcase.

When you arrive unpack the altar and set it up. Light the candle and inhale the scent of whatever fragrance object you've brought with you, letting the fragrance evoke a feeling of thanksgiving for a safe trip. Incense does not need to be lit to be appreciated! Many folks are allergic to the smoke and therefore simply place an entire package of their favorite scent in a vase (stick incense), or on a plate (cone incense), and enjoy the aroma.

Each night while you are away from home, light the candle at bedtime and breathe in the scent of your altar. The fragrance will relax you if you've had a busy day of business meetings. It will evoke gratitude for yet another fun-filled day if you are on vacation. Or if you are one of those folks who hate to fly and spend much of your trip worrying about how you will ever get back on that plane, use the scent to calm you as you envision yourself serene and tranquil on the homeward bound flight. Rather than letting your anxiety about plane travel ruin your trip, let this evening ritual replace your fear with peaceful feelings, by planting in your mind the image of a safe trip. It's easier to envision an uneventful flight while in the peaceful atmosphere of your room, secure on terra firma. On the day you travel, carry the scented object in your pocket or carry-on bag and, before takeoff, let the scent bring you back to that calm place you've visited each evening while you've been away. Relax and enjoy the flight home.

If you forget to bring along the ingredients for an altar, you can create one when you arrive at your destination. It's easy enough to buy a small scented candle and put a snapshot of your loved ones next to it, propped up against the base of the bedside lamp. Light the candle at bedtime and send your blessings to those you love.

If you are on a business trip and concerned about a presentation you'll be giving, buy some fragrant flowers and put them on your travel altar. The evening before the meeting, light the candle and inhale the scent of the flowers while picturing yourself as self-assured at the meeting. Part of the secret of scent is you automatically breathe more deeply while in the presence of a delicious aroma and deep breathing is a relaxation technique. Repeat this ritual the next morning and head to your meeting relaxed and confident.

Any of the above travel altars can be transformed into spiritual altars by the addition of a picture or small statue of a religious figure, or goddess, or angel. This becomes a reminder to maintain your spiritual practice while traveling and to keep a philosophical perspective when things go awry, as they do on every trip.

The Blessingway

labor

I carry a vessel of sacred water

flesh curls in my belly until tides of pain

push me open I heave moan   give way to my

unfolding daughter

1997

This altar and ritual are an adaptation of a Navajo ceremony called the Blessingway, in which friends and relations gather to prepare the path of a person about to make an important journey or passage. In this instance the way is being blessed for a woman who's expecting her first baby. The baby's grandmother plans this ceremony as a way to help her daughter make the transition into motherhood. The women she invites are all mothers who know her daughter well.

On the night of the ceremony the mother creates the altar by spreading a baby blanket on a table set up in the center of the living room. On the altar cloth she places a large bowl, a pitcher filled with spring water, a white lace tablecloth, folded and put at one corner of the altar, an unlit white candle at the second corner, a bowl of rosewater at the third, and a picture of the mother-to-be as a baby at the fourth corner. In the center she places a large bouquet of flowers.

When the guests have arrived, the mother begins the ceremony with these words:

We are gathered here to bless the way for my daughter, _____,

as she travels the road toward motherhood. We are all mothers

offering our wisdom, love, and caring. Let's begin by showering

our blessings on her by each spritzing her face and head with a

little rosewater.

Each woman dips her hand into the bowl, then flicks droplets of rosewater onto the mother-to-be, while offering a blessing aloud. At the conclusion of this initial part of the ceremony the daughter's face is glowing and her hair radiates the scent of roses into the warm room.

The mother now lifts the pitcher and pours a little water over each woman's hands, catching it in the bowl below. While the mother moves from woman to woman, she speaks to her daughter in a clear confident tone:

The energy of our willing hands infuses this water

with strength, courage, and patience, qualities

you'll need during the hard work of labor.

As the mother completes the circle, she places the bowl before her daughter and says,

Take this water home with you this evening. When

your labor begins the midwives will use this water to

moisten the facecloths that soothe your brow. As the

water cools and comforts you, you'll feel our support

in a most tangible way.

Now the mother asks her daughter to stand and shut her eyes. She drapes the lace tablecloth over her daughter's head like a veil.

We who are already mothers will lead you three times

around the altar. Keep your eyes closed; let us guide you.

Lean on us. We offer our support now and, especially,

after the birth of your baby.

At the conclusion of the third turn around the circle the mother stands behind her daughter and with a quick, dramatic movement she grabs the edge of the veil and snaps it off her daughter's head. The startling "crack" of the veil surprises everyone.

_____ , *the abruptness of the sound signifies the profound*

change which will occur within you, once your child is born.

There is no way to prepare you for the mix of terror and won-

der you'll feel. However, we are always there for you as you

experience the joys and the sorrows of motherhood. We are all

mothers—come to us, call on us, lean on us.

The mother-to-be lights the candle and the ceremony ends with each
woman warmly embracing her. Then all gather in the dining room for a special
dinner. The candle glows as the centerpiece on the dinner table. It draws all the
women into its soft circle of light.

9

inspirational inventory:
a summary

Using this summary any woman can create her personal

altar by selecting one item from each list and combining

these pieces in an imaginative way.

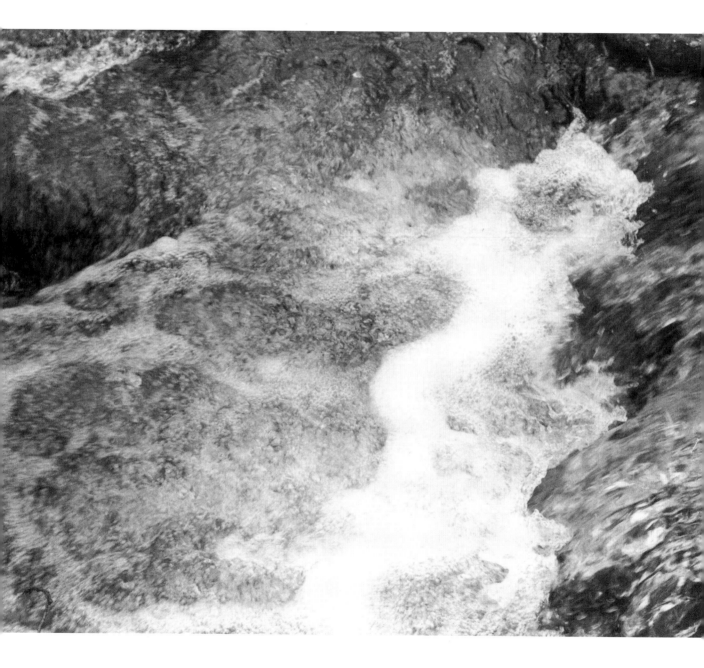

1. Intentions for Creating Altars:

Find inspiration

Honor Mother Nature

Connect with the energy of one of the four elements:

> Wind
>
> Fire
>
> Earth
>
> Water

Pay homage to a totem animal or a deceased pet

Gather healing energies for oneself or another

Make a petition

Communicate with a mythological woman

> Deity
>
> Ancestor
>
> Historical woman

Offer Thanks

Draw on the inherent energy of the altar

Create change

Bless the body

Prepare for a difficult task

Purify self or some object

Bring good luck

Connect with the Muse of Creativity

Honor the Lady of the Wild Things

Gather up your dreams

Appreciation of beauty

Pay homage to the holiness of daily life

Draw in abundance

Honor the rhythm of the seasons

Give blessing to the gardens/fields/crops

Praise your sensuality/sexuality

Collect yourself/be still

Perform magic

Anything that is meaningful to you

2. Places for an Altar:

Dresser top

Sideboard

Corner of kitchen

Windowsill

Top of a hope chest

Hearth/fireplace

Mirror

Plant room

Outdoor garden

Earth mound

Tabletop

Desktop

Upside-down pail

Inside a cupboard

Tree stump

Beach

Circle of flowers in yard/woods

Alcove

Grove of trees

Cave

Crossroads

Springs

Meadows

Clearings

Cliffs

Plateaus

Mountains

Any place indoors or out where you feel

    special/find peace/appreciate beauty/feel powerful

3. Things to Place on your Altar:

Candles

Incense

Seashells

Flowers

Gifts

Written petitions

Masks

Musical instruments

Chalice or wine glass

Bowls of water

Statues

Photos

Pictures

Touchstones

Food

Lights

Scarves

Cloths

Banners

Flags

Feathers

Herbs

Gems/stones/crystals

Potting soil

Journal

Tarot cards

I Ching

Anything you'd like to bless/to absorb
      energy from/to purify/to honor/to
      establish a connection to/to
      evoke associations from/to excite
      the senses

4. When to Change your Altar:

Seasonally

At the full moon or new moon

Weekly

When it no longer grabs your attention
      (this is a signal that you've absorbed the
      uniqueness of this altar and need to
      create anew)

Never (permanent altar)

Perpetually changing altar (add to it and
      subtract from it at whim)

5. What to do at the Altar:

Ceremonies of the voice

    sing

    chant

    recite mantra/affirmations

    read aloud, poetry, myth, spiritual writings,

        stories

Connect with the source of your

    inspiration

    divinity

    light

    abundance

Ceremonies of the body

    dance

    decorate with body painting or jewelry

    anoint with water, smoke, or essence oil

    Tai Chi

    Yoga

    Sit quietly and absorb the sacredness of place

Divination

    Tarot cards

    Runes

    I Ching

    Any oracular vehicle

Rituals of the heart

    Prayer

    Meditation

    Contemplation

    Guided Imagery

    Reflection

Rites of music

    Play an instrument: drum, guitar, flute, etc.

    Sound a bell, gong, wind chimes

    Listen to music

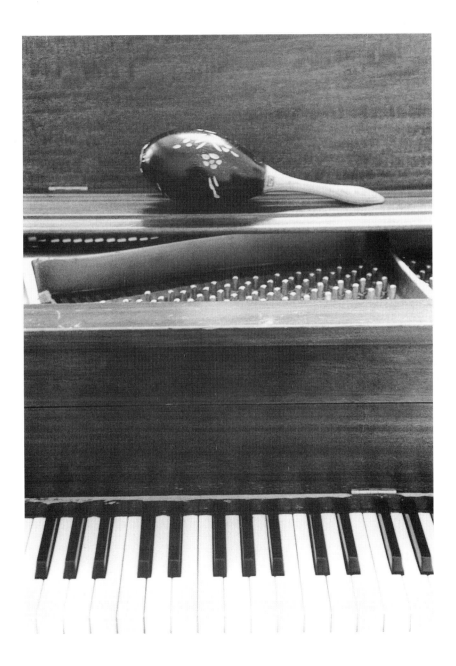

Perfume the air

    Burn incense

    Burn smudge sticks

    Arrange fragrant flowers in a vase or float
        one flower in a bowl of water

    Anoint body with perfume or essence oil

Rituals of writing

    Compose poetry

    Make up your own chant or song lyrics

    Write in your journal

    Repeatedly write the same mantra or
        affirmation

a scrapbook:

my altars

We present these blank pages as an offering to personalize this book with your unique ideas to enhance your altar practice. Jot down themes for altars, compose a poem with an altar as the central image, draw a sketch of your next altar, paste in photos of past altars, add notations about altar music, glue in paint chips and fabric swatches for future altars—anything that will help inspire your altar creations. May your altars shower blessings upon all who see them!

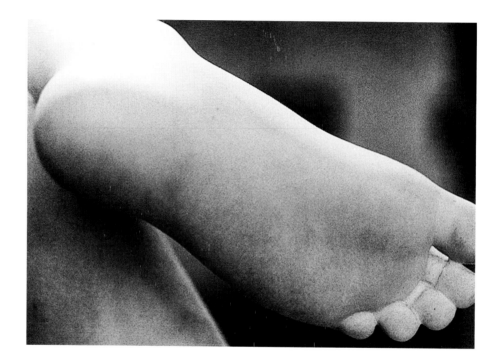

notes

1. Herbal Dream Pillows are available from The Scented Garden, 35 Covell Road, Fairfield, ME 04937.

2. For a fuller discussion of the names of and rituals for the full moons, see Nancy Brady Cunningham, *Feeding the Spirit* (San José, CA: Resource Publications, Inc., 1988), pp. 74-7.

3. For Earth Holidays rituals consult Nancy Brady Cunningham, *I Am Woman By Rite: A Book of Women's Rituals* (York Beach, ME: Samuel Weiser, Inc., 1995), pp. 3-41.

4. Wonderful Kitchen Goddesses can be purchased from: EGODS: The Goddess Factory, founder Sandra Weintrab, P.O. Box 340, Newton, MA, (617) 332-2990.

5. For an in-depth discussion of divination, see Geraldine Amaral and Nancy Brady Cunningham, *Tarot Celebrations* (York Beach, ME: Samuel Weiser, Inc., 1997), pp.84-6.

6. The chant in this ritual is from Margo Adler's workshop at Interface, Watertown, MA, July 1987.

bibliography

Amaral, Geraldine and Nancy Brady Cunningham. *Tarot Celebrations.* York Beach, ME: Samuel Weiser, 1997.

Baldwin, Christina, *Life's Companion: Journal Writing as a Spiritual Quest,* New York: Bantam Doubleday, 1998.

Campanelli, Dan and Pauline. *Circles, Groves and Sanctuaries.* St. Paul: Llewellyn, 1993.

Cunningham, Nancy Brady. *Feeding the Spirit.* San José, CA: Resource Publications, 1988.

————. *I Am Woman By Rite.* York Beach, ME: Samuel Weiser, 1995.

Eclipse. *The Moon In Hand.* Portland, ME: Astarte Shell Press, 1991.

Flack, Audrey. *Art and Soul.* New York: Penguin Books, 1991.

McMann, Jean. *Altars and Icons.* San Francisco: Chronicle Books, 1998.

Medici, Marina. *Good Magic.* New York: Simon and Schuster, 1989.

Monaghan, Patricia. *Wild Girls.* St. Paul: Llewellyn, 2001.

Osmen, Sarah Ann. *Sacred Places.* New York: St. Martins Press, 1990.

Schenck, Deborah. *Fern House.* San Francisco: Chronicle Books, 2001.

Streep, Peg. *Altars Made Easy.* HarperSanFrancisco, 1997.

————. *Spiritual Gardening.* Alexandria, Virginia: Time-Life Books, 1999.

Turner, Kay. *Beautiful Necessity.* New York: Thames and Hudson, 1999.

Wood, Nicholas. *The Book of the Shaman.* New York: Barron's Educational Series, Inc., 2001.